The All About Series
All About ... Canadian Sports

Canada

Curling

Barb McDermott and Gail McKeown
Reidmore Books

Reidmore Books Inc.

For more information contact
Nelson Thomson Learning,
1120 Birchmount Road,
Scarborough, Ontario,
M1K 5G4.
Or you can visit our
internet site at
http://www.nelson.com

Printed and bound in Canada
2 3 4 5   03 02 01 00

We acknowledge the financial support of the
Government of Canada through the
Book Publishing Industry Development Program (BPIDP)
for our publishing activities.

Canada

Canadian Cataloguing in Publication Data
McDermott, Barb.
All about Canadian sports : curling

(All about series)
Includes index.
ISBN 1-896132-49-9

1. Curling—Canada—Juvenile literature. I. McKeown, Gail. II. Title.
III. Series: McDermott, Barb. All about series.
GV845.5.C3M32 1999   j796.964'0971   C99-910772-0

About the Authors
Barb McDermott and Gail McKeown are highly experienced
kindergarten teachers living in Ontario. Both hold Bachelor of Arts and
Bachelor of Education degrees, Early Childhood diplomas, specialist
certificates in Primary Education, and have completed qualification
courses in Special Education. As well, Gail has a specialist certificate in
Reading and Visual Arts, and Barb has one in Guidance.

Content Reviewer
James Lloyd Mandigo, Faculty of Physical Education and Recreation,
University of Alberta

Sports Historian
Dr. PearlAnn Reichwein, Assistant Professor, Faculty of Physical Education
and Recreation, University of Alberta

Credits
Editorial: Leah-Ann Lymer, Scott Woodley, David Strand
Illustration, design and layout: Bruno Enderlin, Leslieanna Blackner Au
Diagram on page 13: Wendy Johnson, Johnson Cartographics

Photo Credits
Cover and stamp photo: Sweep
Magazine
Page
1 Sweep Magazine
3 Sweep Magazine
5 Sweep Magazine
7 Northern Alberta Curling Association
9 Rick Cardella
11 Rick Cardella
15 Northern Alberta Curling
Association
17 Northern Alberta Curling
Association
19 Sweep Magazine

21 Rick Cardella
23 Northern Alberta Curling
Association
25 Rick Cardella
27 Sweep Magazine

We have made every effort to
identify and credit the sources of
all photographs, illustrations, and
information used in this textbook.
Reidmore Books appreciates any
further information or corrections;
acknowledgment will be given in
subsequent editions.

Table of Contents
(All about what's in the book)

Introduction
(All about the beginning)

Sports are games that people play to have fun.

Sports help people to stay healthy.

Sports can teach people how to work together.

Sports are fun to watch.

Curling is 1 of the sports that Canadians play.

CANADA

Curling Is a Fun Sport

Introduction
(All about curling)

Curling is a game played between 2 teams.

Curling is a winter sport that is played at indoor curling **rinks.**

Curling ice is covered with small ice bumps that are called pebbles.

Curling is played with rocks and brooms.

Curlers slide rocks down the ice and try to make them stop on a **target.**

Canad

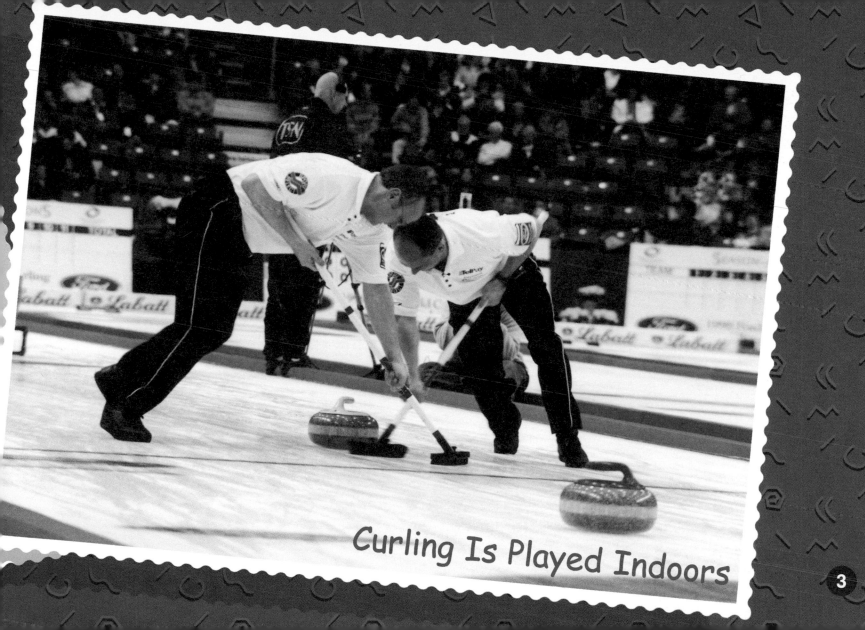

Curling Is Played Indoors

History
(All about how curling began)

Curling may have begun in Scotland or in the Netherlands.

A Dutch artist painted a picture in 1565 that shows a game that looks like curling.

Curling has been played in Scotland for more than 400 years.

A curling rock was found in a pond in Scotland with the year "1511" **carved** into it.

Canad

Curling Has Been Played for 100s of Years

History

(All about how curling began)

Scottish people brought the game of curling with them when they moved to Canada.

Canada is a good place to curl because it has long winters.

The 1st curling **club** in Canada began in 1807.

The 1st curling club was called the Montreal Curling Club.

Today curlers can play in many **competitions,** including the Scott **Tournament** of Hearts and the Karcher Juniors.

Canad

ALBERTA

Canada Has Many Curlers

Uniform
(All about what curlers wear)

Curlers wear clothes that are loose so the curler can move and stretch easily.

Curlers often wear warm sweaters or short-sleeved shirts, pants, and socks.

Curlers wear special shoes.

The bottom of 1 shoe is smooth so the curler can slide easily across the ice.

The bottom of the other shoe has grips so the curler can push against the ice.

Canada

Curlers Wear Special Shoes

Equipment
(All about what is used to curl)

Curlers use rocks that are about 29 cm in **diameter.**

Curling rocks are smooth, round, heavy pieces of stone with a handle on top.

Curlers also use brooms.

Curlers can choose to use **corn brooms** or push brooms.

Curlers use brooms to sweep the ice in front of the rock.

Canada

Curling Rocks

Facility
(All about where curling is played)

Curling rinks are about 43 m long and 4 m wide.

Curling rinks have a target called a house at each end.

A house is 3 circles that are inside of each other.

Curling rinks have a rubber grip called a hack at each end.

Curlers push back against the hack with 1 foot when they are sliding a rock across the ice.

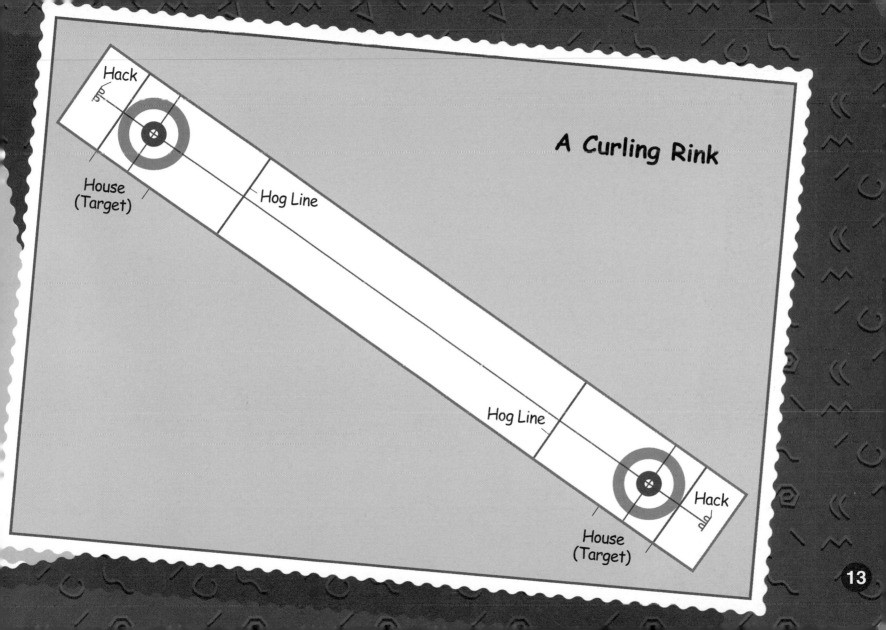

A Curling Rink

Hack

House
(Target)

Hog Line

Hog Line

Hack

House
(Target)

Teams
(All about the players)

Curling has 4 players on each team.

Each player has a job to do during the game.

The skip is the member of the team who helps the other players aim their rocks at the target.

Every player has 2 chances to slide a rock towards the target.

Every player has a chance to sweep the ice in front of the rock with his or her broom.

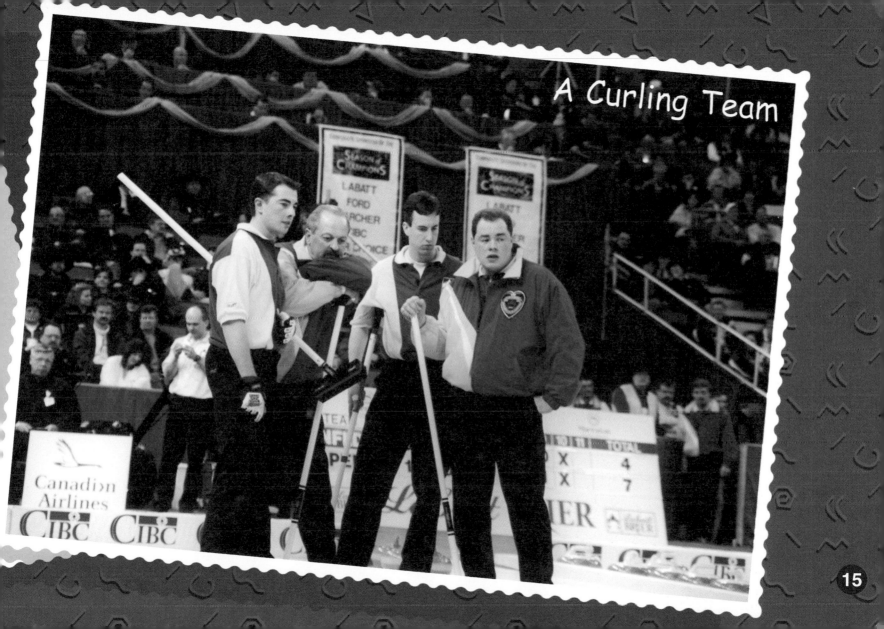

A Curling Team

Rules

(All about how curling is played)

A curling match is divided into ends.

An end lasts about 15 minutes and a curling match usually has 8 ends.

A curling match has 10 ends if the players are **competing** for a prize.

More ends can be added to the match if both teams have the same score.

The team that has the largest score at the end of the match wins.

Canada

Curlers Sometimes Compete for Prizes

Rules
(All about how curling is played)

A coin is flipped before the curling match begins.

The team that wins the coin flip can decide if they want to be the 1st to slide a rock towards the target.

The teams take turns trying to slide their rocks towards the target.

An end is finished when the players from both teams have slid all their rocks.

The rocks are taken off the ice when the end is finished.

Canada

Sliding a Rock

Rules
(All about how curling is played)

Sweeping the ice in front of the rock helps the rock to travel farther and go where it is aimed.

The person who slides the rock aims it at the spot that the skip points to with his or her broom.

The person who slides the rock pushes against the hack with 1 foot and slides down the ice on the other.

Curlers must slide their rock over a line in the ice called a hog line or the rock will be taken off the ice.

Canada

Sweeping the Ice

Rules
(All about how curling is played)

Curlers try to make their rocks stop closer to the centre of the target than the other team's rocks.

Teams score 1 point for every rock that is closer to the centre of the target than any of the other team's rocks.

Curlers try to bump the other team's rocks out of the target.

Curlers watch how quickly a rock moves over the ice so they can decide how fast to slide their rocks.

Curlers watch how straight a rock travels over the ice so they can decide how straight to slide their rocks.

Canada

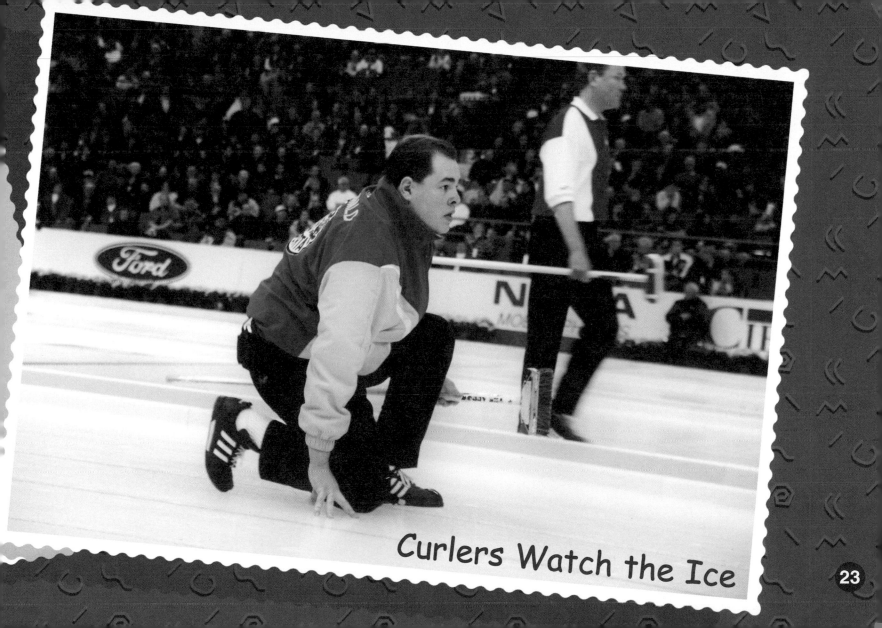

Curlers Watch the Ice

23

Skills
(All about what curling teaches)

Curlers learn how to work with other members of their team.

Curlers learn how to aim their rocks properly.

Curlers learn how to watch the ice so they know how hard to slide their rock.

Curlers learn how to sweep the ice so the rock will go where it is aimed.

Canada

Curlers Learn How to Aim Their Rocks

Summary
(All about the ending)

Curling is a game that Canadians play to have fun and stay healthy.

Curling may have come from Scotland or the Netherlands.

Curlers try to score points by making their rocks stop close to the centre of a target.

Curling is an amazing sport … enjoyed by Canadians!

Curling Is an Amazing Sport

Glossary
(All about what the words mean)

carved (page 4)
Something that is carved has pictures or letters cut into it.

club (page 6)
A club is a group of people who all enjoy the same thing. A sports club is a group of people who enjoy playing the same sport.

competing (page 16)
To compete is to work hard to win something that other people also want.

competitions (page 6)
A competition is a contest where people try to win something.

corn brooms (page 10)
A corn broom is a broom with bristles that look like straw.

diameter (page 10)
Diameter is how wide a circle is. To measure how wide a circle is, draw a line from 1 side of the circle to the other and measure the line. The line must go through the centre of the circle.

rinks (page 2)
A rink is a large area of ice that a sport can be played on.

target (page 2)
A target is something that can be aimed at.

tournament (page 6)
A tournament is an event where many teams go to play a sport. The teams play against each other until 1 team can show that it is better than every other team.